LET'S TALK ABO

FEELING SAD

by Joy Berry • Illustrated by Maggie Smith

SCHOLASTIC INC.
New York Toronto London Auckland Sydney

ISBN 0-590-62387-7

12 11 10 9 8 7 6 5 4 3 2 1   6 7 8 9/9 0 1/0

Printed in the U.S.A.   24
First Scholastic printing, January 1996

Hello, my name is Bonnie.

I live with Eliza.

Sometimes Eliza isn't able to do something she really wants to do.

Eliza feels sad.

Sometimes something Eliza likes very much is lost or ruined.

Eliza feels sad.

Sometimes Eliza has to leave a place she really likes.

Eliza feels sad.

Ms. Berry's room

Sometimes family members or friends leave Eliza.

Eliza feels sad.

When her grandmother died, Eliza felt sad.

When her goldfish died, Eliza felt sad.

When you are sad, you feel very unhappy.

But you don't have to feel sad forever.

There are things you can do to make yourself feel better.

When you cannot do something you want to do, find something else to do.

Then, concentrate on what you are doing instead of thinking about what you cannot do.

When something you like is lost or ruined, be thankful for the other things you have.

Then, use and enjoy these things.

When you have to leave a place you really like, talk with others about that place until you feel better.

Then, find good things about the place you are in and enjoy these things.

When people you love leave you, find out where they are going and how you can reach them while they are gone.

Only contact them if it is absolutely necessary.

Then, keep yourself busy until the people you love return.

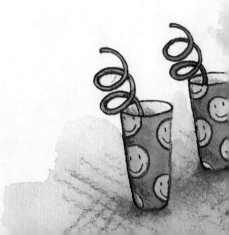

When a loved one or pet dies, cry as much as you need to.

Then, talk with others about the person or pet until you feel better.

It is also good to do something in honor of the person or pet who has died. You might want to do something like draw a picture, write a story, or make a scrapbook.

Try not to hide your sadness.

Don't pretend you aren't sad.

Talk to someone when you feel sad.

Talk as often and for as long as it takes to feel better.

Avoid doing things that make you feel sad.

Try to think happy thoughts.

And, try to do things that make you happy.

Remember that everyone feels sad sometimes.

Feeling sad is okay.

Just be sure to do things that will make you feel better when you feel sad.